Cereal for Breakfast

Cold cereal is a popular breakfast food. You may have had it for breakfast this morning. Kellogg's makes much of the cereal in the United States.

Kellogg's brand cereals come in a wide variety of flavors.

Cereal flakes were **invented** by chance in the late 1800s. Will Keith (W. K.) Kellogg and his brother John Harvey made them.

W. K. was working for his brother when they made the first wheat-flake cereal.

On His Own

W. K. **experimented** to make the cereal better. He used corn instead of wheat. Then he added a little sugar.

W. K. found that sugar made corn or wheat flakes taste better.

John Harvey did not want to add sugar to food. So, W. K. started his own company. It was called the Battle Creek Toasted Corn Flake Company.

W. K. opened his first **factory** in 1906 on Brook Street, behind the San.

Other Cereals

The Kelloggs had gotten people interested in cereal. During the early 1900s, more than 40 companies in Battle Creek were selling wheat-flake cereal.

Battle Creek, Michigan, became known as the cereal capital of the world.

One of these other companies was successful. C. W. Post had stayed at the San. He liked Kellogg's cereal so much that he started his own cereal company.

Post's company, Post Cereal, still makes **cornflakes.**